THE HANDOVER ADVANTAGE

Innovative Door Hardware Strategies to Fast-Track Project Handovers

THE HANDOVER ADVANTAGE

Innovative Door Hardware Strategies to Fast-Track Project Handovers

Ipsa Aggarwal

Available on amazonkindle

Worldwide Published by

Pendown Press

PREMIUM BUSINESS PUBLISHER

PENDOWN PRESS LLP
An ISO 9001 & ISO 14001 Certified Co.,
Regd. Office: 3767A, Kanhaiya Nagar,
Tri Nagar, Delhi-110035
Ph.: 8130886000, 9650072927, 8595249536
E-mail: info@pendownpress.com
Branch Office: 1A/2A, 20, Hari Sadan, Ansari Road,
Daryaganj, New Delhi-110002
Ph.: 011-45794768
Website: PendownPress.com

Edition: 2025
Price: ₹ 399
ISBN: 978-93-7217-943-9

Layout and Cover Designed by Pendown Graphics Team
Printed and Bound in India by Thomson Press India Ltd.

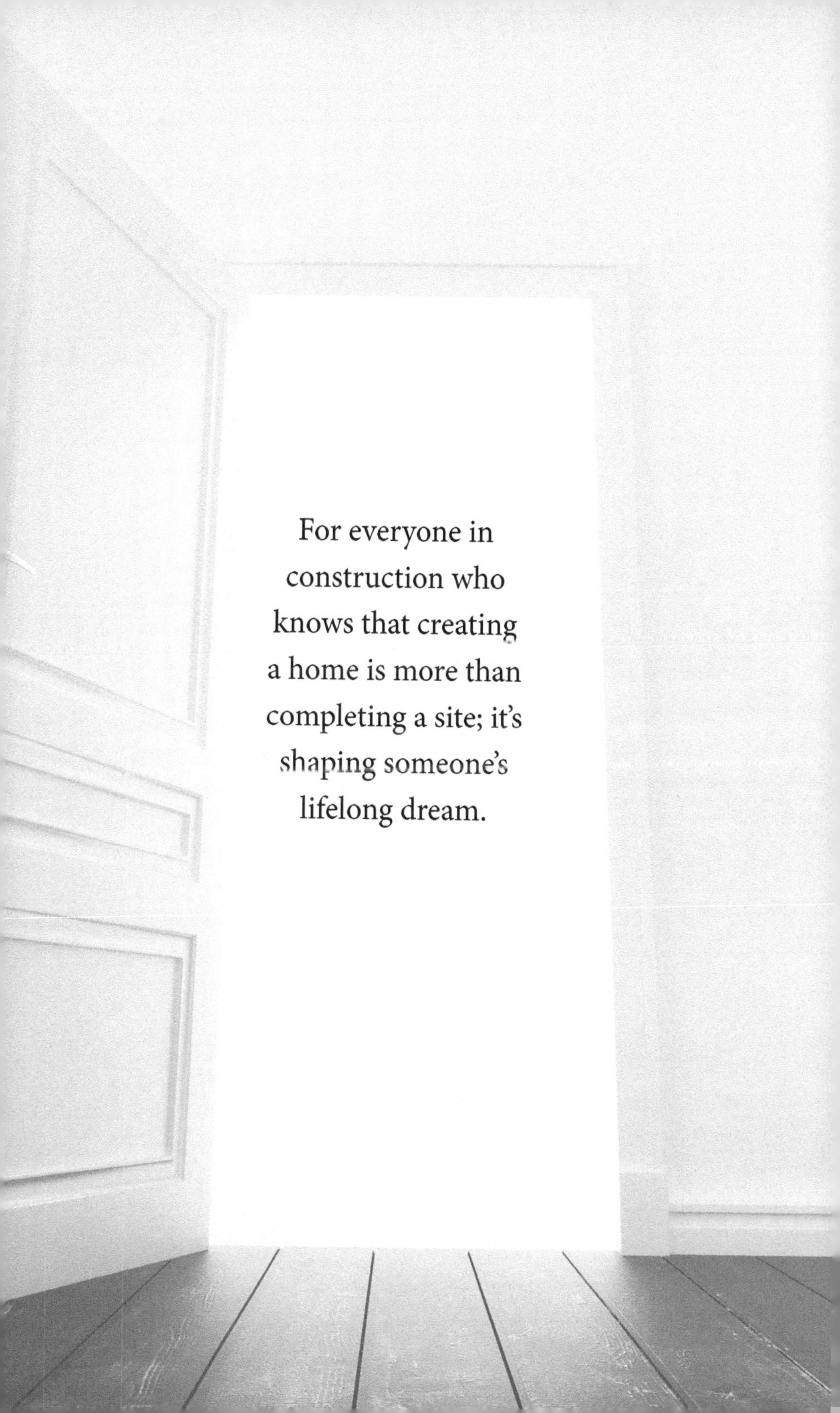

For everyone in
construction who
knows that creating
a home is more than
completing a site; it's
shaping someone's
lifelong dream.

Table of Content

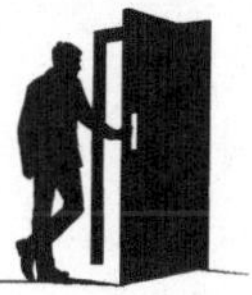

Preface

When I sat down to write this book, I wasn't trying to sound wise or technical. I simply wanted to put into words what I have felt and witnessed for years. Building a home is not easy. It takes time, patience, teamwork and countless decisions. And behind every decision, there is a person trying to do their best.

This book is for that person.

I have seen the stress, the waiting, the follow-ups, the late evenings on site and the pressure to make everything perfect before handover. I have also seen the pride when a project is completed and families walk into their new homes. That moment makes everything worth it.

Sometimes the smallest things get ignored in the rush. Not because they don't matter, but because there is simply too much happening at once. Yet, those small things have the power to make everyday life comfortable or frustrating.

This book was written so that something small doesn't become something stressful later. Not as instructions. Not as rules. Just as guidance.

Thank you for reading. Thank you for caring enough to learn. And thank you for the work you do, because someone's dream becomes real because of it.

Take a deep breath. Turn the page.

We'll go step by step from here.

Acknowledgements

No meaningful work is ever created alone. This book exists because of the people who have walked beside me, supported me, challenged me and believed in me. Every chapter holds a part of you.

To My Parents

Thank you for being my strength. Your quiet confidence in me has shaped who I am. The values you taught me sit between every line of this book. Even when nothing was said, I always felt guided, protected and encouraged.

To My Mentors: Akshar Yadav Sir & Payal Ma'am

You helped me see possibilities I couldn't see myself. Thank you for lending your wisdom and patience, especially on the days when learning felt heavy.

To My Team

You have stood with me through long days, tight timelines and endless revisions. Your faith and commitment turned ideas into something real. I am grateful to share this journey with you.

To Our Clients

Your trust means more than you know. Every discussion, site visit and challenge has shaped my understanding and perspective. Thank you for allowing me to grow alongside you.

To Mr. Dinesh Verma and the Pendown Press Team

Thank you for handling this book with care, professionalism and patience. Your support helped bring these pages to life.

And lastly, to every friend, colleague, and family member who encouraged me, checked on me, or simply believed in me, thank you.

This book may have my name on the cover, but it carries the effort, love and support of many hearts.

With gratitude, always.

My Story

Hello, my name is Ipsa Aggarwal. I am a Door Hardware Strategist. I help builders and developers choose the right door hardware so their projects feel reliable, consistent and worthy of their brand. In short, I help protect reputation through quality.

My connection with this industry goes back to childhood. My name, Ipsa, wasn't just my identity. It was also the name printed on boxes, deliveries, catalogues, and conversations. Whenever I sat beside my father and his phone rang, the first word I heard was my name, followed by discussions grades, sizes, finishes and orders. At events, people often complimented him on the name, and slowly I started feeling proud that something carrying my name was part of people's homes.

There is one memory from childhood that never left me. I had gone to a friend's house for a housewarming celebration. Her younger brother went missing for almost two hours. No one knew where he was. We checked everywhere: every room, the building, the neighbors, the nearby market. Just as fear turned real and someone mentioned calling the police, someone tried to use the washroom and found the door locked from inside. After banging and getting no response, a carpenter was called. The lock had jammed. The boy was inside, scared and crying. The lock had to be cut open.

He was safe. But something inside me changed.

For years after that, I found myself checking locks before shutting washroom doors in restaurants, malls, cinemas and hotels. It became an instinct. A small moment had quietly shaped the way I thought about safety.

In 2020, our company went through a family division. That was the moment I had to decide whether I would step into this industry fully or choose a different path. The decision came faster than I expected. My association with this product, my name, and that childhood incident made the answer clear.

But just joining wasn't enough. I wanted purpose. I kept asking myself:

If I am entering this space, how will I add value? What can I do that goes beyond carrying forward a name?

The answer came slowly but firmly.

Builders create homes. Homes create belonging. And belonging shapes lives.

If I could work with builders, I wouldn't just be selling hardware. I would be contributing to thousands of homes at once. That thought felt meaningful. It felt bigger than just being part of a business.

So I chose to work directly with developers. I chose strategy over selling. I chose education over assumption. And I chose impact over familiarity.

Today, when I see a door open smoothly and someone walks through it without thinking twice, it reminds me why this work matters. It is a small detail, but it affects daily life. A door should never trap someone. A handle should never break when someone is in a hurry. Hardware should quietly do its job so people can live peacefully.

My journey started because of a name. But the purpose came from understanding what that name could stand for.

And now, every time I say, "I work with door hardware," I don't say it as a product line.

I say it as a responsibility.

How I Became a Door Strategist

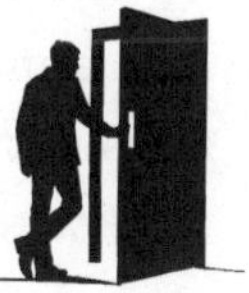

My interest in strategy didn't start in a classroom. It started more than ten years ago when I was given a task without instructions and told to figure it out. Instead of guessing, I spent a month with every department in the company. I wanted to understand how things moved, where delays happened and how decisions were made. That experience taught me something important. Strategy is not theory. It is clarity.

But curiosity doesn't stop once it starts. I wanted to know how big brands built loyalty, how they created demand and why customers waited for them instead of the other way around. So I spent a month thinking about what my next step should be. I wanted exposure. I wanted to learn from people who were already operating at scale.

At a conference in Germany, I met someone who had built a large business empire. We spoke. He offered me an internship. In that moment I remember thinking: this is the door opening. So I took it. And from that point, internships became a pattern. Each one gave me a new way of thinking and a better understanding of structure, communication and consistency.

Eventually I worked with Fortune 500 companies like Novartis, Pfizer and Royal Caribbean. I studied their product launches, marketing decisions and go-to-market strategies. I understood how they executed ideas and why their systems allowed them to scale. After that, I shifted my focus to SMEs in the UK and applied those same frameworks in smaller setups. Seeing those strategies work in real life confirmed something. The size of the business doesn't matter. The clarity of the process does.

Today, I use the same mindset with builders. The product may look small, but a door handle is the first physical interaction a person has with their home or space. Whether it's a hotel room, office, hospital room or apartment, the experience begins there. If the handle wobbles or sticks, the impression shifts. And impressions travel faster than we think.

You might wonder why I chose to share all of this in a book instead of turning it into a paid program or workshop. I could have, but I didn't. Not because strategy isn't valuable but because it isn't used enough.

There are two reasons I am giving this openly.

- **First,** strategy is often ignored in places where it matters the most. People rush decisions, especially for "small things," and later spend time fixing what could have been prevented. When strategy becomes part of the early decisions, the later stages feel lighter and more organised.
- **Second,** I want everyone to select and install the right hardware because even today, buying a home is the biggest dream most people have. And a person lives that dream once every single day. Something as simple as a handle should never feel like a compromise inside that dream.

So if this book helps even one person make better choices, then sharing it freely is worth it. The journey so far has been interesting, challenging and meaningful. And this is just one more step in it.

Why This Book? 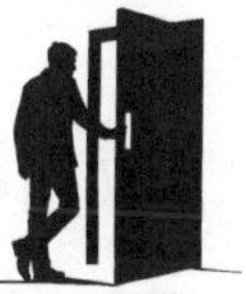

During my visits to procurement teams, one thing became very clear. They are always working, handling pressure, and managing multiple projects at once. Every decision passes through them, no matter how small. Even a nail goes across their table. Their choices shape the project and, in a way, their name becomes part of the building forever. That kind of responsibility isn't small. It deserves support.

In most projects, there are hundreds of decisions to make along with constant coordination. When it comes to hardware, I want to make that decision easier. The right metal, finish, fit and function matter. Even though many of the people I meet have more years of experience than I do, I still want to add whatever value I can, even if it is just one useful point.

Over the last two years, after speaking with around 70 developers, I noticed something. The challenges are the same everywhere. That made me realise that if I truly want to help 10,000 builders globally by 2030, personal meetings alone are not enough.

So I explored ways to reach more people. One of those ways is this book. It lets me share learning, mistakes, insights and solutions at scale.

If one decision becomes smoother because of what you read here, then this book has done its job.

Who Is This Book For?

This book is for developers, procurement teams and project leads who build apartments, villas and large residential communities. It is for those who buy in bulk but still want their project to feel different and well thought out. If you want fewer after-sales complaints, smoother handovers and hardware that doesn't become a headache later, then you are the reader I had in mind.

Many developers I meet have a common goal. They want solutions that are cost-effective, reliable and scalable, without compromising experience. They want hardware that works every day, not something that needs constant fixing after possession.

At some point, we all realise that without a handle, a house is just a closed shell. That small piece of metal decides how a person enters their home. It welcomes them at the end of a long day and protects them when they rest. We have been in the hardware industry for more than forty years and we take that responsibility seriously. Even though we started working directly with developers only a few years ago, the trust we have earned is built on consistency, not noise.

Everyone at Pioneer works with one thought in mind. The product they are building will become part of someone's dream home. A home built with patience, sacrifices and years of effort. That is why, for us, a handle is not just a product. It represents security, comfort and peace.

A home can stand for generations. Hardware should do the same. And if something ever goes wrong, support should be easy and dependable. That has been our belief since the beginning and it continues today.

So if you are someone who builds homes and wants your decisions to age well, then this book is for you.

Now, let's not wait any longer and begin the journey.

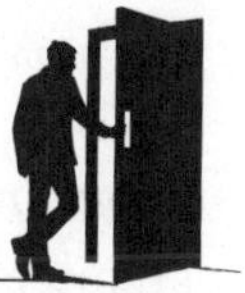

Chapter 1

The Invisible Hero of Every Project – Door Hardware

Step into any new home. Fresh paint on the walls, sunlight pouring through glass windows, the smell of new beginnings lingering in the air. The family standing behind you looks around with excitement, silently hoping this place is where their future memories will live. But before they admire the beautiful interiors or explore the rooms, there is one moment that decides how they feel about the entire home:

Their hand touches the door handle.

If it turns easily, welcomes them inside with a smooth click, comfort flows, confidence rises.

But if it resists, makes noise, or slips loosely?

That single second can cast doubt on everything else the home promises.

Door hardware never asks for attention.

It is small, modest, and often underestimated.

Yet it is the first and most frequent interaction any homeowner has with their space.

"Just like you have one focus: completing your project beautifully, we too have one focus, and that's hardware. Bas hardware."

In our industry, we celebrate what meets the eye. We highlight architecture, amenities, tiles, and textures. Hardware, on the other hand, sits quietly in procurement sheets, usually under the category of "minor items." But in truth, it is not minor. It is a **daily experience,** a **constant touchpoint**, and sometimes, the difference between peace and panic.

Project teams know this story better than anyone. Months of planning, thousands of decisions, endless coordination, and then comes the final stretch: handover. This is where stress peaks, timelines compress, and even experienced professionals feel the pressure.

There is a famous industry truth:

The last 5% of work creates 95% of the stress.
And that last 5%?
More often than not, **it's door hardware.**

A few scratches on handles.
A latch not aligning properly.
A lock that suddenly refuses to perform.
Keys mismatching.
Paint entering the mechanism.
Installation rushed with untrained hands.

Everything is almost perfect, but **one loose handle** can hold up a full building handover. It may cost a few hundred rupees to fix the hardware, but it costs crores in delayed reputation.

Buyers don't remember the struggle behind timelines. They only remember the handle that didn't work on the day they arrived with their family and a box of sweets. They may forget the brand of tiles used, but they will always recall the sound of a door that didn't shut properly.

A project earns its respect not only by looking premium... but by **feeling premium**. And hardware defines that feeling.

Because what is a home?

- A place where parents feel secure.
- A place where a child grows up turning that handle every day.
- A place that holds the dreams and savings of a lifetime.

Every time a handle turns smoothly, the home silently says, *"You're safe here. You're welcomed."*

Every time a lock fails, that dream shakes.

Hardware doesn't appear in brochures.
It appears in **everyday living.**

From the 1st day a buyer steps in to the 1000th time they close the door behind them, hardware protects the experience.

In our four decades of working with hardware, we have witnessed countless success stories and some stressful lessons. And each one taught us the same message:

Small things become the biggest things if ignored.

Hardware is not a product. It is a promise.

- A promise that the home will function smoothly.
- A promise that trust will not break at the turn of a handle.
- A promise that when families step into the next phase of their life, the door will open with ease, always.

Developers want a handover that feels fulfilling and proud.
Project teams want peace of mind after the final key exchange.

Buyers want everything to work, perfectly.

Hardware ensures all three.

So this chapter begins with a simple reminder:
When hardware works, everything else shines.

Key Takeaways

- Hardware is small in cost, but large in impact on user experience and perception.
- A smooth, reliable handle creates confidence during handover and long after possession.
- The final stage of a project often depends on details that are easy to overlook — especially hardware.
- Treating hardware as a planned decision, not a finishing task, prevents last-minute stress and protects reputation.

Chapter 2

When a Door Slows the Next Step

"When a company makes 50 products, hardware becomes a side department. But for us, it's the heart of everything."

Every project moves forward in layers. First comes the foundation, then structure, then finishing, and finally the fine details that make the space livable. Hardware falls into that last stage, not the beginning, not the middle, but the part where things finally start looking complete.

And this is also where timing becomes sensitive.

Hardware doesn't stop an entire project, but it can delay the **next step**, especially during the finishing and handover stage where everything needs to align smoothly.

Where the Pressure Shows

As handover approaches, the project looks nearly complete from the outside. Walls are painted, tiles are polished, lights are working, and doors are installed. But when someone finally tests the hardware; a loose handle, a jammed latch, a missing screw, or a scratched finish can pause the flow.

Not the whole project.

Just the next task.

Painters hold back touch-ups. Cleaning teams wait. Quality audits pause. And suddenly, one small detail becomes part of a chain reaction.

The cost isn't dramatic chaos; it's repeated returns, follow-ups, and time slipping quietly.

How Small Issues Multiply

On a checklist, a scratched handle looks harmless. On-site, it means:

one replacement → one technician visit → coordination → refixing → rechecking.

It is never just a replacement; it's the **cycle** around it.

Most causes are familiar:

- Packaging removed too early
- Wrong screws used
- Finish damaged during painting
- Lock tested late instead of early

These aren't technical failures. They are timing and sequencing gaps.

Training and Timing Matter

Hardware is usually installed while other trades are still active. Without proper planning:

- Handle alignment gets disturbed
- Locking plates get paint marks
- Keys disappear into drawer chaos

And when something isn't right, teams begin the back-and-forth:

"Yeh kab fix hoga?"
"Kaun karega?"
"Kis ne damage kiya?"

It is rarely about blame; it's about clarity.

Nearly **80% of these delays** come from a lack of trained installation teams and unclear workflow sequencing, not from the hardware itself.

The Redo Loop

Once a mistake enters the system, the loop begins:

Identify → Report → Replace → Reinstall → Inspect again.

No one plans for this loop, but almost every site experiences it at some point.

And the real effect?

Not time lost in bulk.

Time lost in **patches.**

What Happens When the System Works

Now imagine another scenario:

- Packaging designed for site handling
- Clear labeling
- Right screws with every product
- Installation done at the correct stage
- Early audits instead of last-minute discovery
- One accountable team from delivery to handover

Suddenly, hardware doesn't slow the next step, it supports it.

That is the advantage of specialization: **clarity over confusion.**

At Pioneer, our internal approach is simple:

Respect the hardware.
Install it right.
Stay ready to support.

Someone once joked:

"Last 5% sabse mushkil hota hai."
Our response was:
"Tabhi hum yahi par sabse zyada dhyaan dete hain."

A Real Example

In a recent project with more than 2,000 doors, something stood out. Not the scale, but the calmness of the finishing stage.

(We all know the usual scenario: Hardware always comes with the right fittings, but many times they aren't used. Installation is often done by contract labour, and they usually pick whatever screws or parts feel quick and convenient. It saves time in the moment, but it isn't always the correct method.)

In this project, the hardware also came with the correct fittings, but this time, the installation team was trained.

Snagging was planned early.
Support was proactive instead of reactive.

Was everything perfect? No.
But the follow-up loop didn't happen.

The handover wasn't rushed; it was smooth.

What's Truly at Stake

When hardware slows the next step, the delay may be small, but the experience isn't. It affects:

- Workflow discipline
- Team confidence
- Customer experience
- And ultimately, the impression of the project

A good installation means the last stage of construction feels organized, not stretched.

And when done right?

A door doesn't cause stress.
It becomes the first smooth welcome into a finished home.

Key Takeaways

- Hardware is small in cost, but large in impact on user experience and perception.
- A smooth, reliable handle creates confidence during handover and long after possession.
- The final stage of a project often depends on details that are easy to overlook — especially hardware.
- Treating hardware as a planned decision, not a finishing task, prevents last-minute stress and protects reputation.

Chapter 3

The Cost of "Cheap" Peace

Every project reaches a stage where numbers sit across the table and quietly start influencing decisions. The BOQ is ready, comparisons begin, and suddenly one supplier looks more attractive than the rest, not because the product is better, but because the price is lower. The difference may look harmless. A few hundred rupees here, a few thousand there, multiplied across a project, it feels like a win.

But here's the truth of our industry:

Money saved in procurement often becomes money spent during handover, after-sales, and brand repair.

That is why we often tell teams:

"Many brands offer hardware as a price card. We offer it as a promise card."

Because the cheapest option rarely ends up being the most economical choice in the long run.

When Savings Come Back as Stress

On paper, saving ₹ 200 or ₹ 300 on a handle sounds reasonable, especially when ordering for thousands of homes. But hardware isn't a decorative element; it's a functional component that is touched, used, turned, pushed, pulled, twisted, and relied on every single day.

And when that cheaper handle becomes loose, or when the lock mechanism wears out early, the small saving becomes a large problem, not just in cost, but in coordination, time, labour, replacements, frustration, and reputation.

Soon the conversation shifts from:

"We saved money."

to:

"We need to fix this — urgently."

And fixing always costs more, financially and emotionally.

The Hidden Question No One Asks: Will This Product Last?

Procurement decisions often end once the product is installed. But the **real test** of hardware begins after handover, when the home becomes lived in.

Today's homeowners are more informed, more vocal, and less patient with inconvenience. They know what they paid for, and they expect every detail to work, especially something as simple as a door handle.

This brings us to a critical question that many teams overlook:

Will this exact product, model, and finish still be available after 5 or 10 years?

Because hardware isn't purchased once, it needs continuity.

Think about these real on-ground situations:

- A bathroom latch breaks after four years; can the same model be replaced?
- A digital lock access card is lost, is the brand still operational?

- A kitchen knob gets damaged, does a matching replacement exist, or will the customer live with mismatched hardware?

These may seem like small situations, but for the customer, they feel like **broken promises.**

And when customers feel ignored or unsupported, complaints don't stay private, they travel:

- On social media
- In RERA submissions
- In builder review forums
- In society WhatsApp groups
- Or even in the conversations between relatives and friends

In the real estate world, reputation isn't lost through one big mistake; it's lost through many small unresolved ones.

The Risk Before the Owner Even Moves In

Another challenge with cheaper hardware is that it rarely survives the construction environment.

Between installation and handover, dozens of things happen:

- No protection on the hardware
- Polish or paint gets applied to the hardware due to lack of protection
- Hardware gets scratched during carpentry or flooring
- Parts go missing from site storage
- Site dust settles on the hardware and starts dulling the finish over time
- Untrained labour forces fittings into place

By the time the apartment is ready for inspection, multiple items need replacing. And replacements always take more time and more coordination than the first installation. That's when the email loops and phone calls begin between the site team, store, purchase and vendors, often over things that could have been avoided with the right process.

Cheap hardware rarely comes with systems.
Good hardware is designed not just to *perform*, but to *survive the journey to performance.*

Life-Cycle Cost vs. Purchase Cost

Hardware shouldn't be evaluated only for how much it costs at the time of purchase, but how much it **prevents you from spending later.**

Purchase cost is what you pay once.
Life-cycle cost is what the hardware demands from you over the next 5, 10, or even 20 years.

Life-cycle cost considers:

- Replacement probability
- Wear and tear
- Finish durability
- Spare availability
- Warranty responsiveness
- Customer experience
- Support structure

And when you look at the entire picture, the cheaper option often becomes the more expensive one.

The Emotional Cost, The One Not Seen in BOQs

When hardware fails, it doesn't just trigger a replacement request; it triggers stress.

Someone has to:

- Track the complaint
- Identify the issue
- Check warranty
- Contact the supplier
- Arrange new hardware
- Schedule labour
- Revisit the home
- Close documentation

A ₹200 saving suddenly becomes dozens of messages, calls, follow-ups, and unnecessary urgency.

Time gets wasted.
People get frustrated.
Teams get blamed.

And reputation gets questioned.

How Pioneer Reduces Future Headaches

Over decades, we've learned something simple:

Builders don't only need hardware, they need **reliability.**

That's why we ensure:

- Stable product continuity
- Matching spare availability
- Training to installation teams
- Durable finishes

- System-based packaging
- Responsible after-sales support

Because when hardware works, nobody notices it and that is the best compliment it can receive.

A handle is not just a functional part of a door. It is the jewel that completes it, something that feels right in the hand, looks right to the eye and works right every time.

Supplier vs. Partner

There's a meaningful difference:

Supplier	Partner
Sells product	Protects brand
Fits into BOQ	Fits into lifecycle
One-time transaction	Long-term support

That's why we often remind procurement teams:

You're not buying for today; you're buying for the next decade of someone's home.

Cheap Hardware Isn't Expensive. Fixing It Is.

So the real question isn't:
How much does hardware cost?
The real question is:
How much will it cost if it fails?

Hardware decisions reflect not just technical judgement, but respect for the customer's lifelong investment.

Because homes aren't built for inspections.
They're built for lives.

And in those lives, every door, every day, should open smoothly.

Key Takeaways

- The cheapest hardware often becomes the most expensive over time due to repairs, replacements, and complaints.
- Hardware should be selected based on lifespan, spare availability, and continuity, not just price.
- Poor hardware choices create recurring delays, rework, and reputation risk far beyond purchase savings.
- Long-term support, stability, and lifecycle planning matter more than a temporary price advantage.

Chapter - 4

40 Years of Listening, Not Just Selling

"Some say we should have expanded into more lines. But we found meaning in depth, not in display. Hardware is not our product; it is our prayer."

Every business has a beginning, and ours started long before product catalogues, smart locks, testing systems or builder partnerships existed. It began with a single decision and a man willing to start from scratch.

Where It All Began

In 1985, my father moved from Punjab to Delhi with hopes bigger than the resources he had. Like many first-generation entrepreneurs, he tried different businesses before finding the one that felt right. His days in Chawri Bazaar became the turning point. That is where **Pioneer** was born, not as a brand, but as an intention.

Back then, we were traders. We sourced hardware from various manufacturers and sold it through the market. If a customer needed something, we found it and supplied it. There was no brand identity, no manufacturing setup, and almost no focus on design or experience. The industry itself was young. People bought hardware as a commodity, not as an element of comfort or emotion.

But slowly, a realisation came.

Hardware wasn't just metal. It was responsibility.

A Brand Was Born

Over time, my father realised that trading could only go so far. If we wanted to deliver consistency, reliability and trust, we needed our own brand. Something that stood for commitment, not just product supply. That is how the name Pioneer came into existence.

It wasn't chosen because it sounded big. It was chosen because it represented courage, the courage to start first, to do something new, and to lead the way, even when no one was watching.

But even with a brand name, something was missing.
We could not control quality.
We could not control production timelines.
We could not control finishes, consistency or long-term dependability.
And most importantly: we could not control experience.

So in the early 1990s, around 1993, we took the next big step. We started our own manufacturing plant. It was not a glamorous setup. It was a beginning, a commitment that if we wanted to build something meaningful, we needed to build it ourselves.

How Pioneer as a Brand Has Evolved Over the Years

1986

Pioneer begins as a hardware shop in Chawri Bazaar, Delhi.

1989

Launch of the Pioneer brand with a focus on quality-first hardware.

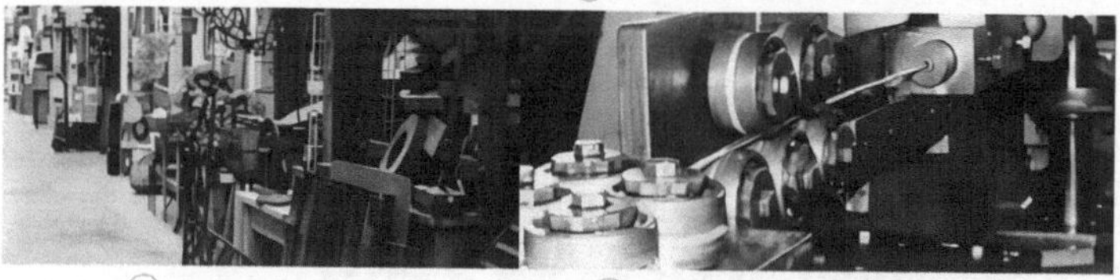

2005

Begins exporting to neighbouring South Asian countries.

2010

In-house electroplating plant launched for premium, long-lasting finishes.

Depth Over Display

Since then, Pioneer has expanded multiple times. New machines, new departments, new materials and new product lines came in, but one thing never changed:

We did not chase being a company of fifty products.

We chose to become specialists.

For us, hardware was never "just another product." It was a responsibility. Something that touches someone's life at least twice a day, when they leave home to chase their dreams, and when they return to rest with their loved ones.

Some people asked why we never expanded into unrelated categories.

The answer was always simple:

"Humne hardware ko business nahi, apni zimmedari banaya."

Because when something protects a home, it should be made with intention, not convenience.

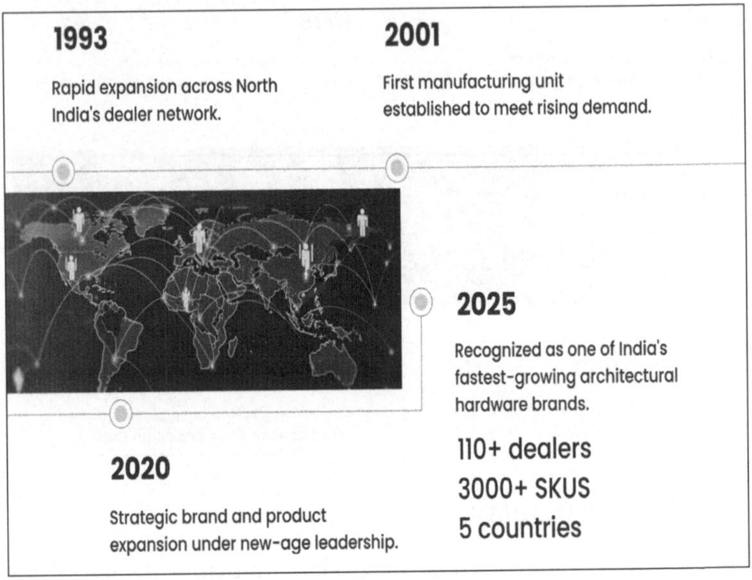

Milestones That Built Us

Over 40 years, Pioneer has grown from a small Chawri Bazaar supplier into a legacy manufacturer trusted across India. Some milestones shaped this journey:

- **Founded in 1985, a 40-year legacy built with consistency**
- **First to introduce moisture-resistant channels in India**
- **99.99% quality compliance across more than 100 projects**
- **Presence across 10 states**

- **More than 3 million users interacting with our hardware daily**

But numbers alone do not tell the story.

Legacy is built when people remember how you made them feel.

And that brings us to the present, where my role enters the story.

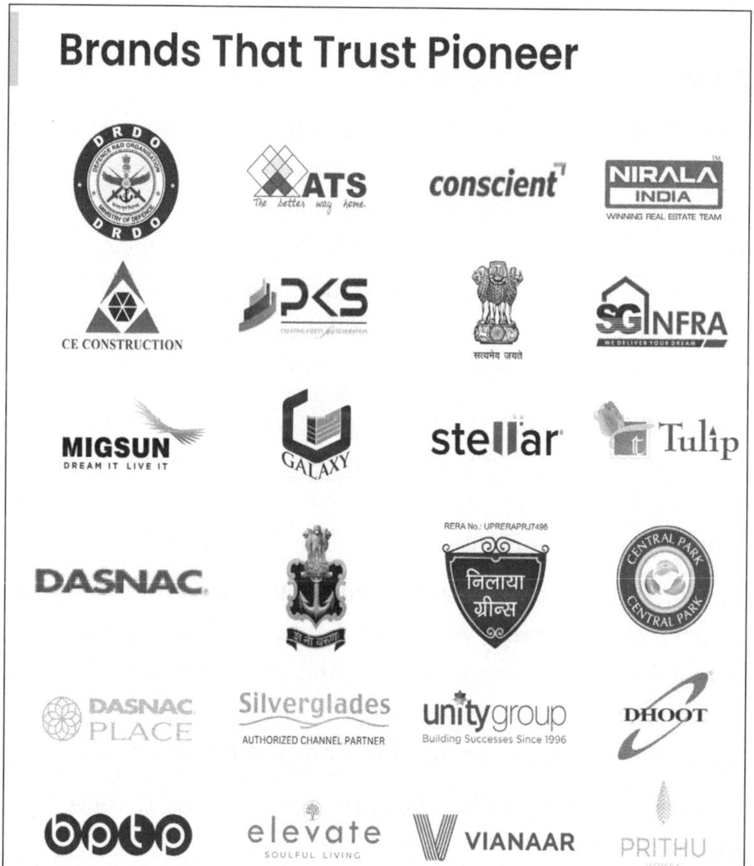

And some more...

- M3M
- Ramprastha Greens
- Signature Global
- Real Anchor
- Civitech
- Strategic
- Aditya Group

A New Lens: Strategy Meets Experience

Like I shared earlier, my path into this business wasn't direct. Before stepping into the world of hardware, I spent almost five years consulting for companies in the US and UK, including several Fortune 500 brands. Strategy became second nature to me. I learned how companies think, how they build loyalty, and how decisions shape user experience long before a product reaches the market.

After COVID and our family business division, I joined Pioneer full-time. But I didn't join only to continue what already existed. I joined to bring a strategic way of thinking into an industry where hardware is often seen as just a product.

Today, when I meet a client, I genuinely enjoy the interaction. I never walk in with the goal of selling something. Instead, I listen. I observe. I try to understand what the project needs, who the end user is and what problem we're trying to solve. My approach is always solution-first, not product-first.

The truth is, hardware is not just purchased; it is chosen for someone's lifestyle.

A digital lock might be exciting for a tech-friendly buyer but overwhelming for an elderly resident.

A slim designer handle might look elegant but may not survive heavy use in a high-traffic building.

So hardware has to match:

- the user
- the door
- the lifestyle
- the environment
- the emotion

A handle should not just fit the door.
It should fit the person opening it.

That is where my strategy background and the real-world experience of this industry meet.

Not in selling, but in designing solutions that make life easier, smoother and more thoughtful for the person who will touch that handle every single day.

More Than a Product, A Touchpoint

When someone visits a project, they notice landscapes, lighting, amenities and architecture. But when they enter their home, the first thing they physically interact with is the handle.

Eyes see the flat. Hands experience it.

A homebuyer may not remember the brand name, but they will always remember how it felt when they opened the door to their first home.

And that experience matters, deeply.

Because buying a home is not a casual purchase. It is years of hard work, sacrifice, and hope.

A handle should respect that.

Hardware as a Solution, Not an Item

When the focus shifts from what is sold to what is solved, the industry elevates.

A handle is not a SKU.

It is an experience shaped by:

- usage patterns
- lifestyle
- security requirements
- ease of access
- environment
- sensitivity of users

And above all: **Reliability.**

My vision is simple: **hardware should simplify life, not complicate it.**

If a person cannot lock their home securely, their entire day is affected. No matter how beautiful the interiors are, or how advanced the digital systems are, if the door cannot close properly, life pauses.

Electricity failing is inconvenient.
Water stopping is frustrating.
But a non-working lock is identity-stopping, you cannot leave, you cannot rest.

That reality drives how we design, refine and test.

Growing With Purpose

Alongside function, sustainability matters to me. Before joining the business, I worked with a social consultancy focused on designing sustainable and socially responsible products. That experience shifted my thinking.

Today, when we develop products, I constantly explore:

- Can this material be more environmentally friendly?
- Can waste be reduced?
- Can we extend product lifespan through smarter design?
- Can we minimise replacements by improving durability?

Hardware has a long-term impact on lives, and it should have a minimal negative impact on the environment.

Why Builders Will Always Be Our Priority

Builders shape cities. One decision impacts thousands of families. Working with builders allows us to create meaningful change faster because scale multiplies impact.

One project may have:

200
500
2,000
or even **10,000 homes.**

Each home represents a life. A routine. A family. A dream.

And when hardware works perfectly, life flows effortlessly.

That is the impact I want to create.

Not louder products.
Not bigger catalogues.
But quieter reliability.

A Promise Passed Hand to Hand

Over forty years, Pioneer has grown, evolved and adapted. But our foundation hasn't changed:

- Listen first
- Understand deeply
- Build responsibly
- Stand behind every promise

Our legacy isn't just the brand.

It is every hand that installed our product.
Every home that opened with trust.
Every client who believed in us.
Every user who never had to think about the handle, because it simply worked.

This business did not grow from selling.
It grew from listening.
And that is how it will continue.

Because in the end:
We are not here to close deals. We are here to open doors.

Key Takeaways

- Hardware quality improves when a company focuses on specialization rather than expanding into unrelated product lines.
- Having in-house manufacturing helps maintain consistency in finish, performance and standards across batches.
- Clear communication between design, procurement, manufacturing and site teams prevents errors and reduces rework later.

- A reliable hardware partner supports the full lifecycle: selection, installation, maintenance and replacement, not just supply.

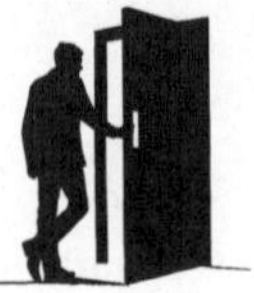

Chapter 5

Calm Handover Code – 7 Stages of Stress-Free Execution

There's a phrase every project head silently wishes was always true:

"When hardware performs, humans relax."

Because the difference between a tense handover and a peaceful one is rarely about big elements, it's about whether the smallest components work as expected without surprises.

We often hear people say, *"You can't predict the last stretch of a project, something will always come up."* But we believe something different:

"Delivering a project on time is not luck. It's process."

When there is a system behind selection, installation, testing, and training, hardware stops being a point of uncertainty and becomes a point of confidence.

Why a Process Matters

The handover phase exposes everything that wasn't tested, checked, or controlled earlier. A door that doesn't close properly, a handle that shakes, a lock that jams, these aren't just technical faults. They create stress, delays, and last-mile coordination chaos.

That's why the only way to avoid final-stage firefighting is to prevent the fire from ever beginning. And prevention needs structure, not assumptions.

Our Calm Handover Code exists for one reason: **To make sure hardware is never a problem at the final stage.**

It isn't complicated. It's consistent.

Stage 1: Appearance Conformity Test - Because the First Impression Matters

A buyer may not know the internal mechanism of a lock, but they notice scratches, dents, uneven polish, and sloppy finishing instantly. This test is visual, but not superficial. Hardware is checked for:

- Uniform finish
- No visible defects or dents
- Smooth edges
- Proper alignment of plates and components
- Consistency across multiple pieces

This stage ensures that when a customer touches a handle for the first time, it feels premium, not like something that was rushed or compromised.

A beautiful structure with flawed finishing creates doubt. A flawless finish creates confidence.

Stage 2: Coating Thickness & Alcohol Test - Ensuring the Finish Stays, Not Just Looks Good

Looks alone don't guarantee durability. Coating thickness is scientifically measured to ensure the metal surface is protected against:

- Moisture
- Daily usage
- Cleaning chemicals
- Rusting
- Scratches

After measurement comes the **Alcohol Test**, where controlled friction is applied repeatedly to verify whether the coating holds or fades.

If it doesn't survive a few minutes of controlled stress in testing, it will not survive years of real living.

Stage 3: Tape Test - The Quick Reality Check

This is a simple but revealing stage.

A high-adhesion industrial tape is applied firmly on the surface and then pulled away sharply. If particles, flakes, or coating peelings come off, the product is rejected.

Why?

Because peeling finish isn't just a cosmetic issue, it becomes:

- Warranty claims
- Angry customer feedback
- Negative site experience
- Replacement hassles

This fast test prevents slow regret later.

Stage 4: Dimensional Stability Check - Precision That Prevents Problems

Hardware may be small, but every millimetre matters. This stage measures:

- Length
- Width
- Screw distance
- Plate alignment
- Rod diameter
- Installation tolerance

If dimensions vary even slightly across batches, installation becomes unpredictable, leading to misalignment, jamming, or operational failure.

Builders expect standardisation.
Buyers expect smooth functioning.
Dimensional discipline ensures both.

Stage 5: Zero-Variation Weight Check - The Hidden Indicator of Material Authenticity

Weight tells a story no brochure can. If two handles of the same model do not weigh the same, it means:

- Material purity changed
- Casting quality varied
- Manufacturing consistency slipped

Variations in weight lead to variations in performance, especially over time.

A zero-variation weight standard ensures every batch matches the same quality benchmark, today, tomorrow, and years later.

Stage 6: Cycle / Functionality Test - Because Hardware Lives in Motion

A door handle should work not for a hundred rotations, but thousands. This stage simulates **real-life usage**, testing:

- Torque
- Movement smoothness
- Spring strength
- Latch retraction
- Lock engagement
- Lever return

Not once.
Not twice.

But repeatedly, to ensure that the experience on Day 1 remains the same on Day 1,000.

Hardware should never feel tired.

Stage 7: Salt-Spray Test - The Long-Term Weather Check

India has varied climates: coastal, humid, dry, industrial, and polluted.

Salt spray testing exposes hardware to a controlled corrosive environment to predict how it will age in real homes over:

- Monsoons
- Daily cleaning
- Moisture exposure
- Environmental pollutants

If a handle rusts, discolours, or reacts to this test, it won't survive years in a customer's bathroom or main door.

This stage protects both, aesthetics and durability.

Beyond Testing: Making Installation Foolproof

Even perfect hardware fails when installation isn't guided.

That's why the process doesn't end with testing, it continues at the site.

60% Faster Installation Systems

Standardized screws, packaging formats, labelling, and fitment documentation ensure that installation is not dependent on trial and error, but follows a repeatable method that saves time and prevents mistakes.

A system is always faster than improvisation.

PioneerFitWale: Training the Hands That Install

Products are only as good as the hands that install them.

Our on-site PioneerFitWale teams train workers and supervisors, not just in installation, but in:

- Handling
- Storage
- Cleaning
- Alignment
- Pre-handover checks

They conduct **pre-installation and post-installation audits**, ensuring everything functions smoothly before the customer arrives.

Because training doesn't just improve execution; it creates ownership.

Reducing Chaos With Installation Kits

Every flat receives a dedicated installation kit, labelled, standardised, and complete. No mixing, no guessing, no missing parts.

This one step alone reduces site-level confusion by almost **80%.** When teams don't have to run around searching for screws, plates, or keys, they finish faster and with confidence.

Or as we often say on-site:

"Jab door chalega chalega, tabhi toh dikhega achha."

From Stress to Satisfaction

When a system replaces unpredictability, the entire tone of handover changes. Instead of rushed calls, re-checks, and panic fixes, the handover becomes structured, calm, and confident.

Hardware stops being a problem.

It becomes invisible, doing exactly what it was meant to do.

Silently. Consistently. Reliably.

Key Takeaways

- A smooth handover happens when hardware is tested early, not discovered late.
- Training installers prevents most of the hardware issues seen during finishing.
- The right system removes confusion and turns finishing work into routine, not firefighting.
- A structured approach saves more time than speed ever will.

Chapter - 6

Service, Installation and Coordination - Reducing the Follow-Up Loop

Hardware failures rarely start because the product is poor. Most of the time, they happen because the installation was done incorrectly, information was incomplete, or there was no structured support system during implementation. In large projects, where multiple teams, subcontractors and timelines overlap, coordination becomes just as important as product quality.

This chapter focuses on a practical reality:

Hardware problems rarely occur in isolation; they occur in the communication gap between the vendor and the site.

Where the Breakdowns Usually Begin

After product selection and delivery, the site expects everything to move smoothly. But issues often begin when installation starts. Typical conversations sound familiar:

- "The screws don't match."
- "This lock isn't fitting."
- "Nobody told us there was a right and wrong direction for installation."

- "The door weight is more than expected, the hinge is failing."

These situations create a cycle of calls, texts, visits, and rescheduling.

The core issue is not always the hardware;

it's the absence of a structured process for installation, training and communication.

Why Installation Method Matters More Than Most People Think

Hardware arrives with the correct fittings. But in many projects, installation is performed by contract labour. They often choose shortcuts, not intentionally, but because they're used to working with generic hardware.

Common examples include:

- Using random screws instead of the ones provided
- Fixing a handle before the door alignment settles
- Removing protective packaging too early
- Applying polish or paint directly on installed hardware
- Installing hinges without considering door weight or frequency of use

These decisions may save minutes during installation, but they increase the chances of failure later.

Once the issue appears, the follow-up cycle begins.

The Solution: Treat Installation and Service as Part of the Product Lifecycle

To reduce avoidable follow-ups, hardware needs a structured service system, not a reactive support model.

A smooth model includes:

- **Installation support (initial phase)**
- **Training for on-site teams**
- **A single communication channel**
- **Technical documentation (spec sheets, door weight guidance, torque requirements)**
- **Scheduled quality checks (pre-finish and pre-handover)**

When these components are planned ahead, hardware becomes predictable rather than problematic.

Reducing Follow-Ups: Practical Steps That Work

Here are proven operational approaches that help avoid repeated complaints and back-and-forth communication.

1. **Request a Technical Supervisor During Initial Installations**

   When new hardware is introduced, having a trained technician on-site for the first few days ensures the team installs correctly. This prevents recurring alignment issues, incorrect fittings, and avoidable rework.

2. **Schedule Regular Check-Ins**

   Rather than waiting for issues to arise, define checkpoints, for example:

   - After first installation batch
   - Before polishing
   - Before final handover

   A 30-minute review prevents hours of correction work later.

3. **Share Technical Specification Sheets**

   Every handle, hinge, or lock performs differently based on the door and user. Specifications such as:

   - Door thickness
   - Door weight
   - Screw length
   - Alignment requirements
   - Minimum hinge count

   help the installation team make correct decisions.

4. **Use Installation Videos When Available**

   Short visual guides help teams work consistently, especially when new labour joins mid-project.

Small Example, But Common Scenario

A concealed hinge is supplied for a premium flat. The hinge is correct, the quality is right, and the design suits the project. But nobody notices that for heavy doors, an additional hinge is required. The team installs only two. Within a few days, the door alignment drops.

The hardware wasn't at fault; **the missing information was.**

Why a Service System Reduces More Than Just Complaints

With structured processes, the impact is measurable:

- ➢ Fewer repeated visits
- ➢ Faster resolution time
- ➢ Reduced back-and-forth communication

- Fewer escalations
- Lower installation errors
- Improved resident satisfaction

Instead of multiple teams calling each other, the process becomes:

one message → one record → one accountable response.

Key Takeaways

- Most hardware failures come from installation gaps, not manufacturing issues.
- Clear communication, technical documentation, and trained installation teams prevent repeated complaints.
- A structured service system reduces time, confusion, and rework, especially during handover.
- Standardised support saves effort for both the vendor and the site team.

Chapter - 7

Designing Hardware That Performs, Not Just Look Good

When most people think of hardware design, the discussion begins with finish and appearance. But in real project environments, design is much more than aesthetics. It impacts usability, durability, maintenance effort and long-term reliability. A handle may look premium, but if it doesn't match the user profile, door weight, climate or usage frequency, it will eventually create problems, even if the material quality is good.

Hardware may be a small component, but its design influences usability, safety and long-term reliability.

Where Design Decisions Go Wrong

Many design choices are made at catalogue tables, not at the project site. As a result, mismatches occur because the selection process considers only appearance, not variables such as:

- A slim designer handle installed on a heavy door becomes loose within months.
- A matte finish chosen for a dusty environment becomes difficult to maintain.
- A concealed hinge selected without checking door weight leads to sagging.

- A premium smart lock provided in a property with tenants results in frequent misuse.

None of these failures are about product quality; they come from design mismatch.

What Should Drive Design Decisions

A good selection process considers key practical parameters:

1. **Door Type and Weight**

   A heavier door requires stronger mechanisms, additional hinges, and handles with proper torque balance.

2. **User Profile**

   If the space will be used by children, elderly people or tenants, the hardware must be simple, sturdy and easy to operate.

3. **Usage Frequency**

   Main entry doors, common area doors and high-traffic access points need stronger components compared to internal bedroom doors.

4. **Environment**

   Exposure to moisture, cleaning chemicals, dust or coastal air impacts finish selection and material choice.

   When these points are considered in advance, design supports durability — instead of working against it.

Material Selection Must Be Practical

Different materials perform differently:

- **Brass:** durable, stable and suitable for premium or long-term projects
- **Zinc:** balanced option for majority of residential projects

- **Aluminium:** lightweight and suitable for low-traffic internal doors

The correct finish also depends on usage and maintenance. A glossy finish may look premium but show fingerprints. A textured surface may be easier to maintain in high-use environments.

Ergonomics: The Part Most People Forget

Hardware is touched every day, sometimes multiple times. The handle should feel stable and comfortable, not sharp, slippery or flimsy.

Practical factors include:

- Comfortable grip diameter
- Lever angle
- Weight balance
- Movement smoothness
- Solid feel when operated

A handle should operate naturally without effort. If a handle feels awkward during the first interaction, it will not improve with time.

Standardisation: A Practical Advantage

One key factor often overlooked is **standardisation across the project**. Using too many models or finishes may look interesting but creates long-term challenges:

- Spare part stocking becomes difficult
- Replacement matching becomes complicated
- Multiple training requirements for installation teams
- Higher risk of mismatch during repair or site movement

Standardisation keeps maintenance predictable and simplifies procurement, installation and warranty handling.

Matching Design to Project Type

Hardware is not universal. Different project types require different design logic:

Project Type	Design Priority
Affordable housing	Durability + easy usability
Mid-segment housing	Balance between cost & reliability
Rental or leased units	Durable, simple, low maintenance
Luxury spaces	Better finishes, smooth operation, long lifecycle
High-traffic zones	Heavy-duty mechanisms and reinforced fittings

The best design is the one that suits the user and environment, not the most visually appealing option.

Future-Oriented Design Considerations

As the industry evolves, hardware design is shifting toward:

- **Modular components** (replaceable parts instead of full replacement)
- **Hybrid automation** (manual + smart options based on user preference)
- **Cleanability** (designs that resist fingerprint marks and surface dullness)

These considerations support long-term usability instead of short-term visual attraction.

Key Takeaways

- Good hardware design balances aesthetics with durability, safety and ease of use.
- Ergonomics, material and usability are equally important as finishes and shape.
- Testing and material matching are essential to prevent future performance failures.
- When chosen correctly, hardware remains functional without frequent adjustments or complaints.

Chapter 8

From Door to Delight – The Future of Project Hardware

The industry is entering a phase where precision, predictability, and user comfort are becoming as important as structural strength. Hardware, which was once purchased towards the end of a project, is slowly moving closer to the planning table. Not because it suddenly became complicated, but because expectations changed.

Earlier, if a door opened and closed, it was considered "done."

Now, people expect doors to feel smooth, operate quietly, align perfectly, and keep performing year after year, regardless of use. And that shift is redefining how hardware will be selected, installed, and maintained in upcoming projects.

The Industry Shift: From Price Decisions to Performance Expectations

Builders are now facing a new kind of buyer: informed, observant, and vocal.

This shift is changing how hardware is evaluated.

Previously, decisions were based on:

- Cost
- Basic availability

Now, decisions increasingly include:

- Technical performance
- After-handover impact
- Standardisation
- Documented traceability

This change isn't driven by trends; it's driven by accountability.

The Real Problem Ahead: Inconsistency

As projects scale, multiple teams, phases, vendors, and timelines overlap. The biggest challenge is not the product itself; it's consistency.

Future challenges will include:

- Different teams installing hardware at different stages
- Replacement difficulty if SKUs change mid-project
- Tracking what was installed in which tower or floor
- Ensuring the same feel and function across units

A building feels premium when everything behaves the same, not when every door feels different.

What Future-Ready Hardware Systems Will Look Like

The next phase is not about new products, but new methods.

Hardware systems will increasingly align with:

- **Standardised SKUs per project**
- **Project-level documentation and mapping**
- **Traceable installation (QR or batch logging)**
- **Defined servicing lifecycle**
- **Uniform operating feel across units**

Hardware won't just be a component. It will be a part of the project's **operational identity.**

A Practical Future Framework: TRACK → INSTALL → VERIFY → SUPPORT

To prepare for the future, hardware planning will follow a predictable framework:

Stage	Purpose
TRACK	Map SKUs to tower/wing/unit. Create traceable documentation.
INSTALL	Use trained teams with standardised fitting steps.
VERIFY	Conduct objective performance checks, not visual acceptance.
SUPPORT	Store service records, spares mapping, and escalation paths.

This ensures hardware doesn't become a future guessing game.

Why This Approach Reduces Risk

A predictable hardware system protects projects from:

- Vendor discontinuation
- Memory-based installation practices
- Spare part mismatch
- Future confusion during renting, resale, or repairs

A building may go through three or four ownership cycles, but the hardware system should remain understandable throughout.

Where 'Delight' Comes In

Delight doesn't come from features.
It comes from predictability.

A door that:

- Opens smoothly
- Feels stable
- Sounds right
- Requires no thought

creates trust.

And when every door in a building behaves consistently, it doesn't just function; it elevates the perception of the entire project.

Key Takeaways

- The future of hardware is consistency, documentation, and repeatable processes, not last-minute product selection.
- A building feels premium when every door operates the same, not when every hardware set is different.
- Standardisation and traceability will become core requirements in large-scale housing.
- Delight comes from predictable experience, not visible complexity.

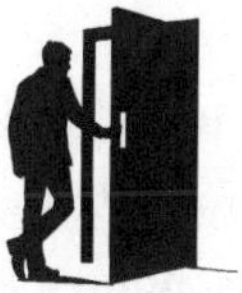

A Door That Opens Both Ways

> "You trust us with your project; we trust you with our life's work."

This isn't just a thank-you note. It's a reminder of the relationship we have built with you over the years. When you choose our hardware for your project, you are not just buying a product. You are placing trust in something we have spent decades shaping, improving, testing, and caring for.

We know your world isn't easy. There are deadlines, unexpected site challenges, shifting plans, and long nights that no one outside the industry ever truly sees. We have lived versions of that journey too, which is why we don't take your confidence lightly.

For us, every door installed is a shared responsibility. The builder, the contractor, the site teams, and us. It is never one person's job. It's a partnership.

If someday a customer opens a door smoothly and doesn't think about it, that is success. If you complete a handover without hardware stress, that is success. If years later the same handle still works the way it did on day one, that is success.

So thank you for choosing us. Thank you for believing in what we build. And thank you for letting our work become a small but meaningful part of the homes and lives you create.

Together, we don't just close doors. We open trust.

Ipsa Aggarwal

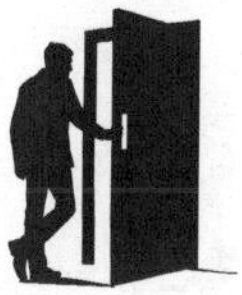

Now, It's Over to You

Thank you.

Not just for reading, but for giving your time, curiosity, and attention to something that often gets overlooked in the rush of construction.

If this book helped you think differently about hardware, handovers, or project planning, even in a small way, then it has served its purpose.

But books are only the beginning. The real value happens when conversations start.

So if you have questions, feedback, or ideas, or if you want to explore how we can work together on your upcoming projects, I'd love to hear from you. You can reach out whether you want a quick clarification or a detailed discussion.

Send me a message, share your thoughts, or book a **1-to-1 call**. I reply personally.

Email: ipsa@pioneeripsa.com

Thank you once again for being a part of this journey.

Let's continue shaping homes that last, decisions that age well, and doors that open to peace, not stress.

Looking forward to connecting.

Ipsa Aggarwal

Appendix

1. Hardware Selection Checklist

Choosing hardware isn't just about matching designs. It's about ensuring long-term performance. Use this checklist before finalising:

- □ Confirm the metal type is suitable for the project environment (coastal, high-traffic, residential).
- □ Check finish durability and test reports (salt spray, cycle testing, coating standards).
- □ Ensure the design is timeless and available for future replacements.
- □ Verify warranty terms and after-sales response timelines.
- □ Confirm availability of spare parts for at least 5–10 years.
- □ Check installation compatibility with door thickness, alignment, and frame type.
- □ Ensure samples are tested on-site, not only in office meetings.
- □ Confirm packaging is site-friendly and protects the finish until handover.
- □ Discuss training support for installation teams.
- □ Ensure there is one single point of contact for coordination.

If every point gets a "Yes," you're selecting more than hardware; you're selecting reliability.

2. Site Readiness & Installation Guide

Smooth installation begins with site discipline. Before hardware is fitted, ensure:

- Doors are fully aligned and painted.
- Moisture content in wood is stable.
- Protective layers remain until handover.
- The right screws and fittings are available for each model.
- Installers are trained and briefed on standards.
- The site has secure storage for spares and extra sets.
- Cleaning chemicals used do not damage finishes.
- Work sequence is followed: carpentry → painting → hardware → final polish.
- Records of installations and issues are logged for easy tracking.
- Final testing is done after installation, not during it.

A prepared site reduces rework, saves time, and ensures hardware performs from day one.

3. Cost of Delay Calculator

Simple thinking framework (no math pressure):

Cheap Product Saving Today:

X saved per door

Possible Future Costs:

Replacement + Labour + Coordination Time + Complaint Handling + Warranty Calls + Reputation Impact

Real Cost:

₹ (X saved) vs. ₹ (rework + labour + stress + time + customer dissatisfaction)

If the future cost outweighs today's saving, even emotionally, it's not a saving. It's a delay waiting to happen.

4. Handover Readiness Checklist (Built With Love)

This checklist ensures the buyer enters a stress-free home:

- ☐ Every handle works smoothly and feels firm.
- ☐ Locks open and close without resistance.
- ☐ Keys are labelled clearly and tested before handover.
- ☐ No scratches, dents, or paint marks remain on fittings.
- ☐ Door alignment and latching are checked twice.
- ☐ All missing items and pending fixes are logged and resolved, not carried forward.
- ☐ Spare keys and warranty terms are clearly communicated.
- ☐ The site is clean, organised, and ready, not rushed.
- ☐ Contact details for after-sales are shared proactively.
- ☐ The final walk-through feels calm, not like inspection.

A good handover isn't a checklist; it's a feeling.

5. Door Hardware Care Card for Residents

To keep your door hardware working smoothly:

- Clean handles gently with a soft cloth.
- Avoid harsh chemicals, acids, bleach, or abrasive pads.
- Do not hang heavy bags, belts, or keys from the handle.
- Check screws once every six months and tighten if loose.
- Ensure kids do not swing or pull the door with force.
- Keep locks lubricated with recommended oil (not random household oils).
- Avoid slamming doors, use door stoppers.
- In case of difficulty, contact building maintenance instead of DIY fixes.

Good care ensures your door feels new, year after year.

Notes

Notes

Notes

Notes